# ALL THE LIGHT I SEE IN YOU

Tahia Zia

BookLeaf Publishing

India | USA | UK

All the Light I See in You

© 2021 Tahia Zia



Presentation by BookLeaf Publishing

Web: www.bookleafpub.com

E-mail: info@bookleafpub.com

ISBN: 9789358360424

First edition 2021

# DEDICATION

For the ones who still believe

In themselves

In the future

And in the World

# PREFACE

A compilation of whimsical thoughts and experiences. That's what this is. This book is a collection of my 'mind and memories', which have helped me many times, and I thought it might help you too. This was unplanned, spontaneous and out of the blue, but sometimes the best things are. The poems to come are for you and me but not for most people. As you read on, you'll notice that they have no titles, just numbers. You create the titles. You find your own meaning. You feel it. Explore, imagine, be curious. It's all up to you. It's all for you. I just hope that you'll use it wisely…

T.Z

# ACKNOWLEDGEMENTS

I came up with the thought of publishing something, anything, around the end of 2020. But I never imagined that within the next year, I would have my first ever publication. While going through the daily highs and lows of teenage life, writing has always been of help, and one day, I thought that if my writing can help someone as problematic as me, then there has to be at least one other person out in the world, who might benefit from it too. As excited as I was, the task seemed very daunting, so I decided to go with what I knew best, poetry. What I hoped to do and what I hope I have done with these poems by the time you have finished them all, my dear reader, is to give you a sense of comfort, hope and inspiration.

I couldn't have done any of this of course, without the amazing editors and the team at Alvira Publishing. You guys turned a dream into reality, and I cannot thank you enough. Thank you to my friends who have been my No.1 supporters and who were first in line to buy this book, even before it was written.

To my family, who have done more for me than any person deserves, thank you for your unconditional love and support. I never told you I was writing something, so… surprise! Thank you for believing in me in everything I do, even if you didn't exactly know what I was doing.

To every person in need of a friend and in search of somewhere to belong who happens to pick up this book, I hope you can rest here. I wrote this for you. Keep on keeping on

Affectionately yours x

You are your strength

You are your power

You are your faith

You are your hope

You are your peace

You are your love

You are your truth

You are your cure

We give pieces of ourselves away

We work tirelessly to build others up

We give and give and give

Yet we never get them back

Life is a tragedy wrapped in a beautiful melody

She was walking on ice

One wrong step and it would crack

And she would fall

Fall deep down

The world around her would crumble to nothing

And she would drown

Drown in her own fears and worries

But the ice is not yet cracked

And so she walks

One step in front of the other

Ever so slow

Ever so gentle

For one small misstep

And it would be the end of it all

Talk to the sun

Maybe even the moon

Listen to their stories

The sun will you tell you that you don't have to shine bright every single day

Sometimes it's okay to stay behind the clouds

And the moon

It'll tell you that it's okay not to show up

To only show a part of yourself

But both will tell you that it's okay to disappear

When things don't go right

Deep into the night

But just always remember

It's important to come back

And spread your light

I want to be the person who checks in and asks how you are going daily

I want to be the person who keeps track of all the things going on in your life

I want to be the person who is right there on the phone listening to you vent after a bad day

I want to be the person who struggles alongside you when it comes to choosing what to wear

I want to be the person who is there to celebrate your highest highs and gently go through the lows

I want to be the person whose shoulder you can cry on

I want to be the person who you call first when you have big news

I want to be the person who you goof around with

I want to be the person who gets into pillow fights with you

I want to be the person who reminds you of all the amazing things you are doing

I want to be the person who helps you uncover your true potential

I want to be the person who reminds you of how incredible you are

I want to be the person who can show you how loved you are

I want to be the person who gives you the biggest bear hugs

I want to be the person who is there for you every day, everywhere,
every time

If we ever fall in love

let's never tell the world

the world tends to ruin beautiful things

so, we'll protect it, and let it be our little secret


If we ever fall in love

let's always keep our promises

I've broken way too many to know they're like cookies

once you break it, everything crumbles


If we ever fall in love

let's be patient

let's take our time and live in the moment

tomorrow's a mystery, and it's better that way

If we ever fall in love

let's never be scared

love is like a trust fall

but we won't fear falling, we'll be there to catch each other


If we ever fall in love

let it be everyday

let's learn, grow and love a little more

each coming day


If we ever fall in love

let's make it an adventure

let's take the leap of faith every chance we get

after all, life's too short to not take risks


If we ever fall in love

let's ride the roller coaster

We'll go through each laugh that makes our stomach ache, and the
pain that makes our heart break

we'll ride the highs and lows, because we can't know one without
the other



If we ever fall in love

and we may never fall in love

but if we ever do, then love me with all your heart

but please, the only thing I ask of you is please don't break my
heart

Embrace your wild emotions

you are allowed to swing

From pure happiness

to being reduced to tears

From raging anger

to complete peace

From absolute frustration

to utter content

Can you imagine

if the fiery blaze

was reduced to the flicker

of a candle?


Or

if the ocean

decided her tides were too strong

and stayed forever flat?


Don't reduce yourself to a lake

when you are as great

as the Pacific Sea

The sun came and saw me

just as she does everyday

but this time it was special.

She cast herself into my window

her rays danced on my floor

the shadows and the silhouettes

painted a curious picture

dark on the inside, but bright all around.

She sat on my windowsill

with splashes of her golden skin

and told me that she was proud of me.

She confessed that she has been watching me from a distance

and she noticed how the lines in my palms

no longer traced the shape of sadness

that once hid inside my hands

or the stormy clouds that we both sometimes hid behind.

She told me that she purposely burned me

during the days in Summer that I spent beneath her

so that my skin would shed

In all the places, where pain had gripped me

so that the layers that have constantly been poked and prodded

could reveal the beauty inside.

She told me that she no longer hears my organs

whisper to each other as I sleep

wondering why they were ever called vital

as I spent days pleading with them

to give up on me

in the same way I had given up on myself.

She stroked me with her warmth

and thanked me for pushing through

for living through the days

where she saw me trying to bury myself

deep inside, and beneath the earth.

She told me that the glow of my smile

made her look duller

than the skies of grey.

She told me I am one of her brightest lights

as she slowly slipped out of my window

and I saw her in all her glory

as she set below the horizon

and as she went, she whispered to me

that the beauty of her sunset

cannot be compared to the beauty of my soul.

And so, I waited for tomorrow

when I would see her once again

just as I do every day.

10

When things go wrong,

something new will come along,

something you never knew could be,

something brighter than the big blue sea,

something that takes you way up high,

something with no limits up in the sky.


It will come from the fires that have now gone out,

it will come from the fires you once knew all about,

it will come from the trenches of your deepest pain,

it will come from the moments you felt you had nothing to gain,

it will come from the roots of your brightest smile,

it will come from the moments you went the extra mile.


And you will rise from the ashes that are now left.

You will rise from the ashes that have been put to rest.

You will rise higher than you've ever gone before,

you will rise with the mightiest roar.

You will rise more beautiful than the sun,

you will rise for your story has only just begun.

Smile

For no reason whatsoever

For no one in particular

Just for you

Smile when your jaw aches from all that laughter

Smile when everything's a bit of a blur with all the tears in your eyes

Smile purely because you want to

Smile just because you need to

Smile because the world craves it

Your smile in particular, lights up every single room you walk into

It's extremely contagious too

So spread it, like wildfire

Smile whenever you can, wherever you can and however you can

Repeat it

Never forget it

Smile so that it becomes muscle memory

Effortless

Smile because they need it more than you'll ever know



and so do you.

You are my chosen family

If it is, let it be,

If it is not, let it rot –

I connected the dots,

all the dots.

I drew a pretty picture,

it was funny and sweet, and made me think of the future,

We could do it together, you and me – what a weird mixture.

They say I'm happy with a smile

So, call me up – let's talk a while

We'll work together – let's go the mile


The facts are laid out for you to see

So, no matter what, just let it be

# 14

"Hand me a pen and I'll rewrite the pain"

I used to feel quite panicked

When dark clouds entered my skies

I knew the sun couldn't always shine

But I just wanted to stay dry


But just like flowers need water

We sometimes need to feel the pain

So I put down my umbrella

And learned to dance in the rain


And I hoped that one day

You will join me out there

When you step out of your shell

And smell the fresh air

Then we will go live our dreams

In a world that knows no pain

And when the drops fall from the clouds

I'll take you dancing in the rain

Though big decisions often leave your heart racing

There is power in standing up for yourself even if your voice is shaking.

In a world that can make you lose your way

There is power in giving it your all each day.

There is power in succeeding when you thought that you couldn't

There is power in loving someone when the world thinks you shouldn't.

When all the weight of the world feels burdened on your shoulders

There is power in having so much strength, you could move boulders.

There is power in remaining soft and still being kind

In a world with so much hatred, it makes you lose your mind.



26



There is power in getting back up when you've been pushed to the ground

And I've realized that big statements and gestures are not the only places where power is found.

If tomorrow starts without me

I hope my mum can find some peace

Knowing that even though my life was short

I lived a lifetime before it ceased


I hope that after they shed their tears

Enough to even mimic the sea

My friends will laugh as their eyes crinkle

When they tell their many tales of me


I hope one day they'll tell their children

About their friend who was wild and free

And how much I would've loved them

And all the fun that I would've been

I hope that my dad will remember

Of all the times I held his hand

And that I was more scared of letting go

And tumbling over on the sand


If tomorrow starts without me

I hope that all my teachers will know

That my future brightened with each lesson they taught

And their words went deep and helped me grow


I hope my family will learn to move on

As the photos bring tears to their eyes

For I'm no longer filling the empty space

Instead I'm soaring through the skies

I hope that all the quiet will be filled

As you sing along to my favourite song

Even though the melody breaks your heart

You smile and keep dancing along


I hope you feel me early in the mornings

When the day has just begun

When you see a sparkle in the sky

As you sit and watch the rising sun


If tomorrow starts without me

And the sun shines without my light

I hope you know how much I love you

And that the happiness I brought you will fly like a kite

And if tomorrow starts without me

Remember we're not that far apart

I'll be your guiding light from above

And I'll always be there in your heart

I often think back to those days

When we were innocent and free

And all those little memories

That will forever stay with me


The photo albums and all the collections

Perfect moments frozen in time

A return trip to moments gone by

Without the cost of a dime


They tell a story, so many stories

Of childhood shenanigans and dreams

When the biggest worry of our day

Was sorting out the cricket teams

Broken windows and concerned neighbours

The usual of our daily lives

The cuts and bruises barely felt

While saving boundaries with concrete dives


Next door, in front, or a couple houses down.

Every household in the colony

Welcomed everyone, new or old

They, were neighbours, friends and family


Long trips to Nan and Pop's

Stuck in traffic as hours go by

Staying up with cousins at night

Watching movies, having fun; how the time would fly

One day, we left all that behind

And travelled far to a foreign land

No more comfort or familiarity

As slowly, a new life began


Now, I've grown up here and learned their ways

Far from home and family and friends

Met new people and learned new things

But the loneliness never really ends


I love it here, I've made it my home

Yet my heart still yearns for the day I'll go back

For I miss my culture and my people

So, when the day comes, I'll be the first to pack

34

Bubble, bubble, do our troubles

Kept inside, they tend to double

It'll bury you within its rubble


So, lift the lid

Slow the boil

A problem shared is half the toil

I woke up early morning, feeling quite chilly and checked the weather to see what it was like.

It said that it'll drop lower than 10°, so, I snuggled up and went back to sleep again.

He got up one morning and felt kind of odd, so he checked the weather to see what was up.

It said that there was a storm that was brewing, but it was down on the streets and what people were doing.

The storm that brew was dark and powerful, leaving devastation in its wake.

As the people committed grave, grave sins while fighting over the colour of one's skin.

She got up one morning while it was still dark outside, as the clouds above blocked the sun.

The weather was cloudy with a chance of rain, but it was the tears of children that would fall once again.

They crashed one after the other, they rained from the skies, as they shivered with fear, not knowing if they'll survive.

Thunder wasn't that common; they would never see lightning strikes. Instead they took cover, as they were battered with airstrikes.

They were walking on a cold, cold day, but it was the sting of the grief that made them shiver.

A whole family has become stars in the skies, as the supremacist brutally took their lives.

I feel the weight of the world on my shoulder, as I get older people get colder.

The values of humanity; compassion and equality, people coming together in unity - leaves hope for a world than could one day be free.